THANKYOU

To all the kids who shared their thoughts. You have made this book special. You matter to us.

WWW.2MILETOOLKIT.COM

Every effort has been made to ensure the accuracy of all narrations.

For more information about this title or to request permission, you can write to contact@2miletoolkit.com

ISBN 9789354266010
Ebook ASIN B08P5NXVL2
ISBN 9781638500698

https://www.2MileToolkit.com/

Dedicated to

Kids around the world.

May you grow in wisdom and understanding each day of your life.

WWW.2MILETOOLKIT.COM

Introduction

What is this book about?

This book reveals a glimpse of what life is for 13 kids from 11 countries during the Coronavirus (COVID-19) pandemic in 2020.

Who is this book for?

Every child has a story to share. If you love a good story, this book is for you.
If you are a parent and have little ones, you can read it to them.

Why was this book written?

I believe it's essential to capture what our young ones around the world think of this pandemic and how they have adapted to the change.
Their story can reach many kids around the world and can be a ray of hope at this time.

When and How were the children interviewed?

I interviewed the children early October 2020, through an online questionnaire. It was conducted after receiving their parents' consent.

What about their identity?

The only identifier disclosed is the name of the child/grade/city/country.

Illustrations used are for representation sake only and do not resemble the child in any manner. It is purely to add flavour to the narration and provide a visual treat.

Author's Note

Dear Children,
You have been a silent bearer to all the changes year 2020 brought in.

It was so quick, yet you remained patient with us (parents and caregivers). It was not easy, but you agreed to walk with us without complaining.

You knew to play your part well. And that's a great encouragement for us grownups.

In this book, I bring together special thoughts from 13 kids around the world.

Let us read further and know more about them and what they want to share with us.

ETHAN

A Senior Kindergartener from Mississauga, Canada and attends school online.

My very first understanding of Coronavirus (COVID-19) was that it attacks you.

Things have changed in my life now. I cannot play in the park anymore.

However, I learned to play more games with my sister. I am looking forward to visit Dino park when the world becomes 'Coronavirus free'.

My message to other kids around the world -
Wear mask 'n stay happy.

IAN

Grade 1, Chicago, USA
attends school online.

I first thought of
Coronavirus (COVID-19)
as some kind of virus that
we need to be careful of.
Life has changed now.

I can't go to swimming class and playground now. During this time, I learned how to ride a bike and play the piano at home.

I'd be happy to celebrate a 'Coronavirus free' world. My message to other kids around the world - Let's have a hope that we can be free from Coronavirus soon!

DEV

Grade 1, Singapore

attends a combination of traditional schooling and online (a.k.a blended learning).

I had no idea what Coronavirus (COVID-19) was. Learnt about it for the first time. My life has changed now. Can't play outside and have to wear a mask always. However, I learned to draw using YouTube.

After the world is 'Coronavirus free', I'll travel everywhere.

My message to other kids around the world - Hang in there.

Anaïs Tartibu

Grade 2, Johannesburg, South Africa attends traditional schooling.

I understood Coronavirus (COVID-19) as a social disease.

Life has changed now.
I can't spend time with my friends.

During this time, I learned to bake.

WOW! after the world is 'Coronavirus free', I will hug my best friend again.

My message to other kids around the world - Let's practice social distance as it's for our own good and please do not forget to sanitise.

AYRA

Grade 2, Islamabad, Pakistan attends school online.

I know that Coronavirus (COVID-19) is a very bad virus and we can get very sick from it.

So I stay often at home and avoid going out. I learnt how to play more indoor games and use more internet-based activities that are for children.

I will celebrate with a big party and invite all my friends when the world becomes 'Coronavirus free'.

My message to other kids around the world - Don't worry it won't be like this forever and it will be better once we have the medicine for this virus.

SHRIYA BHARDWAJ

Grade 4, Abu Dhabi, United Arab Emirates attends school online.

My very first understanding of this new 'Coronavirus'[COVID-19] was that it would attack you if you did not hydrate your throat; by that I mean if you did not drink water over a long period of time.

At the start, this was all I knew about the new virus.

In the past few months, the extraordinary change in our life was that, going outside meant wearing masks and gloves and coming back home meant at least having bath & changing clothes.

Wearing the same clothes again which we wore outside, without washing, was a big NO. Also, I have to take steam and warm water. This was always a 'must' and a rule. I have learned to worship God, and I see it as the best gain in the world.

A "Coronavirus free" world would be a big celebration, and I would always grab the chance to go out freely; no tension of wearing masks and gloves or no bathing after returning home. My message to other kids around the world - We have to beat this so called 'strong' Coronavirus. But this can only happen if we stand together to do so.

Let's get Coronavirus to run out of this world.

RENAE REJI

Grade 4, Navi Mumbai, India, attends school online.

WWW.2MILETOOLKIT.COM

I first thought Covid-19 was a big fearful disease. Life has changed now - there's online school, online talking, mostly being isolated at home & outdoor playing has become less.

I'm taking care of my health by eating healthy foods. I ride my bicycle at times. I find it inconvenient to wear mask all the time.

I learned to tie my hair in a proper ponytail (it's a bit long) and I learned to make Chapatis (that is Indian flatbread).

Because of online schooling, I got to know more about technology. I have to remember to avoid staring at the screen for a long time.

I get to spend more time with my kid sister, and she is eager to attend my online school classes too.

The day the world becomes Coronavirus free, I will enjoy the day and will go out freely.

No mask anymore!

My message to other kids around the world -
Even though we face hard times, we can always ask God for help.

We should make the best of every opportunity we get.

EVA AGNEL

Grade 5, Dubai, United Arab Emirates, attends school online.

I first thought that Coronavirus (COVID-19) was just a normal flu kind and we could handle it. Then when schools, businesses and going out was forbidden, I had changed my mind. It really was a disaster.

At the start of this lockdown, I was pretty happy that there was lockdown because then there was no school. But then they forbade more and more stuff like 'no going out for a whole month or so'.

It was getting boring because I eagerly wanted to go & meet my family (who are away from us) and my friends. Then school started online. And now unlike the olden times, there are so many masks, and wherever we go, we have to first check our temperature.

During this lockdown, I have learnt how to play many board games and have got better at playing the piano. When the world becomes Coronavirus free, I will first have a party and invite all my friends to rejoice that this pandemic is finally over. Then I will go back to my home country and meet my family.

My message to other kids around the world - Stay calm, don't panic, this pandemic is soon going to end.

Johannes Jahmes Altobar

Grade 6, Manila, Philippines attends school online.

I understood Coronavirus (COVID-19) as a very dangerous virus.

Things have changed in my life now. I cannot go outside the house. If I do, I always have to wear a mask and face shield. In these past months, I learned to chat online with my teacher and watch online live teaching. I will be happy and excited to see a 'Coronavirus free' world.

My message to other kids around the world - To stay safe and help their parents at home and help them in house chores.

ADRIAN ALAPATT

Grade 7, Dublin, Ireland, attends traditional schooling.

I learnt that Coronavirus (COVID-19) is so serious that we had to go home for a long time.
Life has not changed much for me. I am back at going to school, except there are restrictions in school.

I have learned cycling and also to cook. I don't want to take things for granted.

My message to other kids around the world - This virus won't be there forever.

ZIDANE & ZANE

Inseparable brothers in Grade 8 and 6 respectively from Floreal, Mauritius, attends traditional schooling.

Zidane: I felt this virus was just prevalent in China. In all that free time I got to exercise and develop some muscles.

I learnt to breathe through a mask.

Me and my brother have learnt to concentrate despite noises from kitchen appliances like grinder and cooker.

When the world is 'Coronavirus free' we will celebrate all day with friends in a fun and activity-filled place.

Zane: Initially, I felt that this virus was a false alarm.
Wearing mask makes me look like a Ninja,
and it added a notch to my style quotient.

I learnt to use Zoom during the break from attending school and we brothers have upped our technological skills because of online classes.

At school, we need to wear our masks and also carry an additional one.

The break timings are different for different grades, so there is no overcrowding. We are often told to use hand sanitizers.

Our football classes have started too.

Our message to other kids around the world - Believe in yourself. Be strong and include exercise in your daily routine.

Jeron Jiby

Highschooler (year 9),
Benalla, Australia,
attends school online.

I thought Coronavirus was just a normal virus and would go away quickly. I did not think at the time it would be such a long stretch.
It certainly over exceeded my expectations.

I definitely got used to being indoors. I really took the outdoors for granted. I had to find things to do inside the house.

I missed a lot of my friends during this time. I feel like I can endure more now, more than what I could 6/7 months ago.

I learnt to cook. I enjoyed baking and I did more of it. I enjoyed it very much because at the end there is a reward - you can eat the food.

I like trying out the different flavours and making creative designs.

After the world is 'Coronavirus free', I would go out more. And spend time with my friends rather than staying indoors and not doing something productive.

It is good to be outside and active rather than sitting indoors all day. I would use my time productively and spend that time with loved ones.

My message to other kids around the world - This is just a phase in the world. We will get through this. Keep your head up and keep pushing.

About the author

Tabitha Reji is an Indie author, professional IT consultant and Early Childhood Educator inspired to design, teach and write for young minds.

As an IT consultant with experience in telecommuting workstyle, she knows what it's like to have a dropped connection, dreadfully slow network, no charging points, noisy background and a pain in the neck.

It sparked off a collection of posts categorized as 'Wisdom@Work' that places a strong emphasis on work style and you. She also shares her experience with children and education at 2miletoolkit.com. She hopes to give valuable insights into child care and learn from children alongside building them up. Her IT and Education sector experience has helped her be mindful about being organized and well prepared. She has also designed numerous planners to help remove the chaos from the day and replace it with a more fulfilled smile.

You can visit her online at https://www.2miletoolkit.com, on Facebook at facebook.com/2MileToolkit/ or write to contact@2miletoolkit.com.

www.ingramcontent.com/pod-product-compliance
Lightning Source LLC
Chambersburg PA
CBHW040749170726
48282CB00019B/103
9789354266010